SO GOOD!

THE INCREDIBLE CHAMPIONSHIP SEASON OF THE 2007 RED SOX

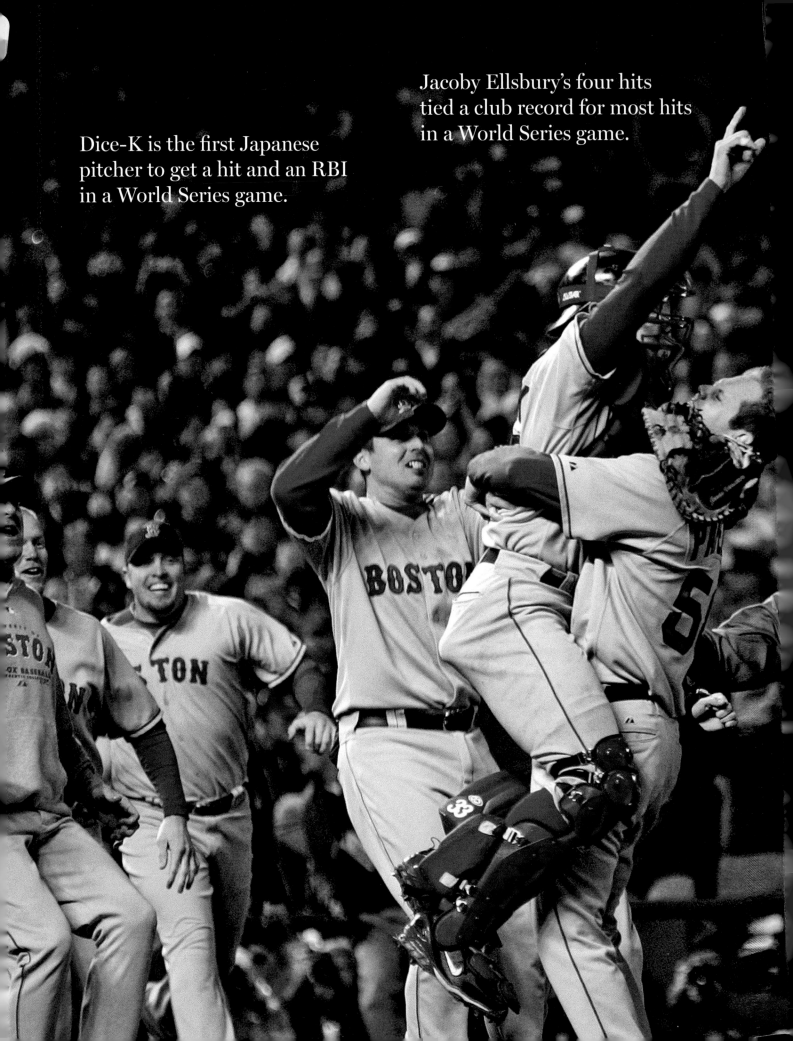

Dice-K is the first Japanese pitcher to get a hit and an RBI in a World Series game.

Jacoby Ellsbury's four hits tied a club record for most hits in a World Series game.

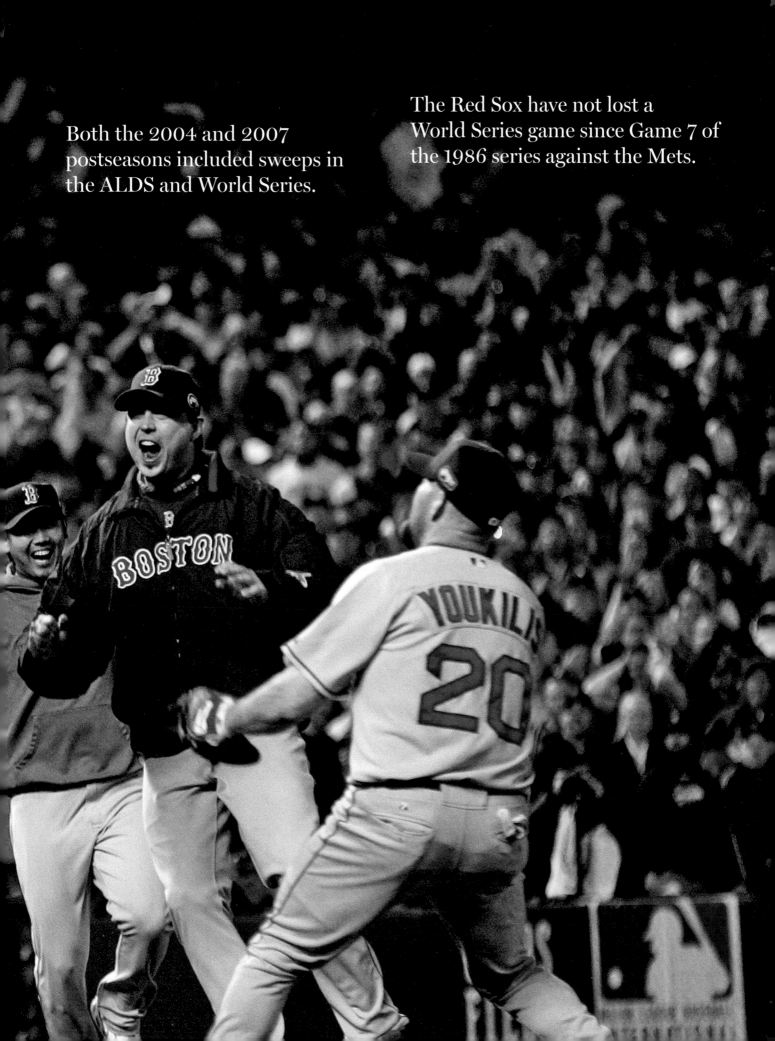

Both the 2004 and 2007 postseasons included sweeps in the ALDS and World Series.

The Red Sox have not lost a World Series game since Game 7 of the 1986 series against the Mets.

The Boston Globe

This book is available in quantity at special
discounts for your group or organization.
For further information, contact:
Triumph Books
542 South Dearborn Street, Suite 750
Chicago, Illinois 60605
Phone: (312) 939-3330
Fax: (312) 663-3557

Printed in the United States of America
ISBN: 978-1-60078-114-8

TRIUMPH
BOOKS

BOOK STAFF

EDITORS Gregory H. Lee Jr., Janice Page
ASSISTANT EDITOR Ron Driscoll
ART DIRECTOR Rena Anderson Sokolow
DESIGNER Jerome Layman Jr.
PHOTO EDITORS Bruce Pomerantz, Jim Wilson
RESEARCHERS Ben Cafardo, Liberty Pilsch,
Bruce Pomerantz
IMAGING Frank Bright, Jeff Dillon,
Cynthia Meloski, Janine Rodenhiser, Richard Smith

PHOTOGRAPHERS

THE BOSTON GLOBE Thushan Amarasiriwardena,
127 • John Bohn, 110, 123 • Yoon S. Byun, 128
• Barry Chin, front cover, 2, 14, 15, 22, 41, 43, 44,
45, 46, 47, 52, 56, 57, 58, 60, 69, 71, 91, 92, 98, 99,
102, 104, 106, 109, 125, 127 • Jim Davis, 1, 9, 12, 15,
18, 19, 20, 23, 25, 26, 27, 28, 35, 38, 39, 40, 42, 45,
48, 49, 50, 51, 53, 54, 59, 67, 68, 70, 72, 73, 76, 77,
83, 84, 85, 87, 90, 91, 92, 94, 95, 97, 98, 100, 101,
108, 114, 120, 122, 124 • Bill Greene, 15, 18, 42, 62,
123 • Stan Grossfeld, 4, 10, 16, 21, 25, 29, 30, 36, 41,
74, 86, 88, 89, 124 • David Kamerman, 104, 105 •
Matthew J. Lee, 90, 91 • David L. Ryan, 84, 122, 126,
back cover.

ADDITIONAL PHOTOS COURTESY OF
AP/Wide World Photos, 97 (Ron Schwane), 111
(Chris O'Meara), 112 (Steve Nesius); Reuters, 96.

With special thanks to The Boston Globe sports
department, photo and design departments, and
library staff.

Front cover Red Sox closer Jonathan Papelbon
records a save during a season in which he earned
All-Star honors. Papelbon was successful on 37 of
40 save chances.

Opposite page Manager Terry Francona and
General Manager Theo Epstein display their team's
latest World Series trophy with pride (top), and
pitcher Mike Timlin shares his bubbly with the
crowd.

Back cover The American League Championship
pennant waves over Boston while being installed
atop the Berkeley Building (the former John
Hancock Tower) on Oct. 24.

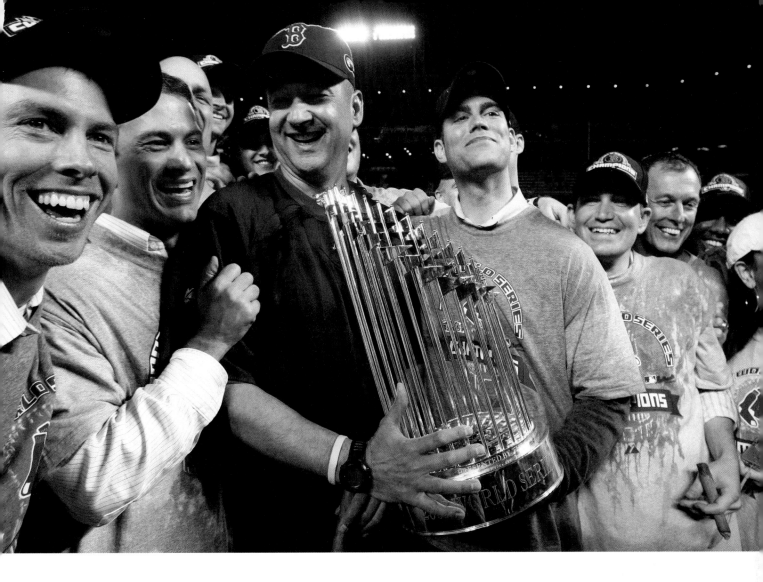

CONTENTS

They won the laughers and the close ones; for the second straight time in the Fall Classic, they won all the games, this time by a combined 29-10 score.

Game 1 • Francis vs Beckett

13-1

	1	2	3	4	5	6	7	8	9	R	H	E
COL	0	1	0	0	0	0	0	0	0	1	6	0
BOS	3	1	0	2	7	0	0	0	x	13	17	0

WEDNESDAY OCTOBER 24, 2007 • **FENWAY PARK** ◇◇◇◇◇◇

Game 2 • Jimenez vs Schilling

2-1

	1	2	3	4	5	6	7	8	9	R	H	E
COL	1	0	0	0	0	0	0	0	0	1	5	0
BOS	0	0	0	1	1	0	0	0	x	2	6	1

THURSDAY OCTOBER 25, 2007 • **FENWAY PARK** ◆◆◇◇◇◇

Game 3 • Matsuzaka vs Fogg

10-5

	1	2	3	4	5	6	7	8	9	R	H	E
BOS	0	0	6	0	0	0	0	3	1	10	15	1
COL	0	0	0	0	0	2	3	0	0	5	11	0

SATURDAY OCTOBER 27, 2007 • **COORS FIELD** ◆◆◆◇◇◇

Game 4 • Lester vs Cook

4-3

	1	2	3	4	5	6	7	8	9	R	H	E
BOS	1	0	0	0	1	0	1	1	0	4	9	0
COL	0	0	0	0	0	0	1	2	0	3	7	0

SUNDAY OCTOBER 28, 2007 • **COORS FIELD** ◆◆◆◆◇◇

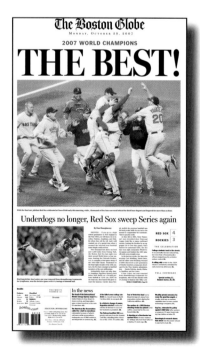

WORLD SERIES

Sox
ROCK

October 29, 2007 • BY GORDON EDES/Globe Staff

DENVER — When it happened the first time, in 2004, Terry Francona was stricken with temporary amnesia. ♦ "I actually don't remember getting out to the field," the Red Sox manager said of a moment burnished deep in New England memory banks. "You wait your whole life for that minute, and I don't know where the hell it went." ♦ A minute that used to recur like a comet, once 86 years or so and missed by generations of Sox fans, is now beginning to feel like a birthright. For the second time in four seasons, the Red Sox are World Series champions, Francona and the rest of the Sox dugout borne onto the grass in Coors Field on October 28 by the same wave of euphoria that struck in 2004. ♦ The Sox completed a four-game sweep of the Rockies with a 4-3 win before 50,041 witnesses, the Rockies succumbing as swiftly as the Cardinals did in '04. ♦ The seventh world championship in franchise history comes in a year in which the Sox were mighty in spring —

leaping to a 10-game lead by the middle of May — and splendid in autumn, sweeping aside the Angels, Indians, and Rockies. ♦ "It's a little different," said Sox general manager Theo Epstein when asked to compare that championship feeling. "It's like comparing your children. You can't do it. But this one was sweet because it was a top-to-bottom organizational effort. So much hard work. It wasn't a fluke. We worked hard to get here." ♦ The Sox join the Yankees as the only American League teams to sweep in successive Series appearances, and the third team overall, Cincinnati doing it in 1976 and 1990. ♦ The Sox won their final seven games of the postseason. Their longest winning streak of the regular season was five. ♦ Jon Lester, the cancer survivor who began the spring in the low minors, brought a lump to the throat with five scoreless innings. "His ability to go out and focus on what he had to tonight, after all that he's been through and the road he has traveled, it's a storybook ending to a great year," said Francona.

WS 1

Colorado outfielders Matt Holliday and Willy Taveras can only watch as a flyball by Boston's first batter of the Series, Dustin Pedroia, tops the Green Monster for a home run and a quick Red Sox lead.

W S ⬥1

Jacoby Ellsbury, who had moved to left field, and Coco Crisp, a late-inning defensive replacement, share a laugh as they make their way in following the final out of the 13-1 Game 1 victory.

 W S 2

Mike Lowell barely beats the throw as he takes third base on a single by J.D. Drew in the fourth inning. The extra base was critical as he scored on a sacrifice fly by the next hitter, Jason Varitek. Julio Lugo (above) lays down a bunt to move Jacoby Ellsbury to second base in the sixth inning. Ellsbury was stranded at third when David Ortiz flied out.

Matt Holliday
chases Mike
Lowell's fifth-inning
line drive into the
left-field corner.
Lowell's double
plated David Ortiz,
who had walked
with two outs and
gone to second
on a base hit by
Manny Ramirez.

310

W S 2

Curt Schilling tips his cap after leaving the game in the sixth inning. In perhaps his final start with the Red Sox, he allowed just four hits and one run and earned his 10th postseason victory. Hideki Okajima (left) and Jonathan Papelbon preserved the victory, although Papelbon was sent sprawling by a Matt Holliday liner in the eighth inning. The Sox closer got the last laugh when Holliday was picked off at first to end the inning.

Daisuke Matsuzaka (top) helped his own cause, first by snaring a comebacker that led the Rockies' Kazuo Matsui to be caught too far off second base, and then by rapping a two-run single (right) in the third inning that extended Boston's lead to 5-0.

Jacoby Ellsbury was a bit of a doubles machine for the Red Sox with three two-base hits, including one (left) that drove in Julio Lugo in the eighth, and one that barely eluded Colorado center fielder Corey Sullivan (above) in the third.

If you go to a high school graduation in New England in the Year 2026, you will hear a lot of Jacobys, Dustins, Jonathans, and Hidekis when they call the roll. And it will remind you of a special time when it seemed the beloved local baseball team simply could not lose.

Five thousand feet above sea level and 1,800 miles from Fenway Park, the Boston Red Sox won their second World Series in four seasons, beating the Colorado Rockies, 4-3, to complete a four-game sweep of the 103rd Fall Classic. Frustrated for the final eight decades of the 20th century, the Sox have emerged as hardball monsters of the new millennium.

Indomitable closer and nifty

dancer Jonathan Papelbon fanned pinch hitter Seth Smith on a 94-mile-per-hour fastball at 10:05 p.m. (MST) on October 28 for the final out, then heaved his glove toward the heavens. Catcher Jason Varitek stuffed the precious baseball into his back pocket while he ran out to the mound to congratulate his teammate. Time to pop the corks.

As they did in 2004, Terry Francona's men shredded their National League rivals like so many cardboard cutouts, beating the Rockies by an aggregate 29-10 over four games. Once famous for autumnal folds, the Sox have won eight consecutive World Series games and finished the 2007 playoffs with seven straight wins.

In the postseason, Sox fans who worship Curt Schilling, David Ortiz, and the other curse-breaking veterans of 2004 discovered a new generation of October warriors; young men developed by the Theo Epstein administration ... Dustin Pedroia, Jacoby Ellsbury, Papelbon, and Jon Lester.

It was Lester, one year removed from chemotherapy treatments for lymphoma, who won the clincher with five innings of shutout ball. Mike Lowell, who hit a home run and a double, was named World Series MVP, and Bobby Kielty's pinch-hit home run in the eighth inning proved to be the difference.

"I'm so proud of Jon Lester," said Francona. "I thought it was very appropriate that he got the win. It's hard to come up with the right words."

After the final out, thousands of Sox fans convened behind the third base dugout and lingered for more than an hour, standing, chanting, and saluting their champions.

That game started with a bang when Ellsbury, the rookie of Navajo descent who started the season in Double A, hit the second pitch of the night into the left-field corner for a double and came around to score on a single by Big Papi. New generation meets old. Same result.

The 23-year-old Lester hadn't started in the majors in over a month. He finished the season in the minor leagues and was not included on the Sox' 25-man roster for the Division Series against the Angels. And then he went out and won the clinching game of the World Series one year after his chemo treatments. Jake Gyllenhaal is already lined up to play the lead in "The Jon Lester Story," a major motion picture coming soon to theaters near you.

Lester gave up three hits and three walks. Manny Delcarmen finished the sixth, but gave up a homer to Brad Hawpe to start the seventh. When Delcarmen put another man on base, 41-year-old Mike Timlin — another holdover from '04 — came on and fanned two of the Rockies' best hitters.

There was stardust sprinkled all over the Sox dugout. Pinch hitting in the eighth, Kielty homered on the first pitch thrown by Brian Fuentes. It was Kielty's only appearance in the World Series.

Papelbon was summoned for the five-out save. Papelbon pitched 10 postseason innings without giving up a run.

Francona, Boston's oft-maligned manager, is 8-0 lifetime as a World Series skipper. And his boss, Epstein — who walked away from the job for a few months in 2005 — has a second championship ring.

"What happened in '04 we'll never forget," said Francona. "But this is '07 and we said that from Day 1 and we accomplished our goal and it's not easy to do."

In October of 2007, the streets of Boston are paved with gold. And for awhile, at least, those streets will be packed with the legions of Red Sox Nation, saluting the World Champion Boston Red Sox. Again.

 Red Sox principal owner John Henry (above) and veteran teammates Tim Wakefield and David Ortiz know how to celebrate a World Series title after Boston captured its second crown in the past four seasons. Goggles have become standard issue as beer and champagne are sprayed around the winning locker room.

A pair of inning-ending strikeouts are punctuated by Red Sox starter Jon Lester (left) and Mike Timlin. Lester fanned Matt Holliday to end the third inning, and Timlin got Troy Tulowitzki in the last of the seventh.

Mike Lowell did his Super-
man imitation as he dove
home with the second run
of the game after Jason
Varitek's single. Lowell hit
.400 in the four-game
sweep with a homer and a
double in the clinching game
to earn the MVP trophy.

W S ◆ 4

Jamey Carroll hit just
two home runs in the
regular season, but
his drive off Jonathan
Papelbon in the last of
the ninth sent Jacoby
Ellsbury crashing into
the wall to haul in the
second out.

The Indians trounced the Red Sox in three straight games, but couldn't put them away, as Boston outscored Cleveland, 30-5, in Games 5 through 7 to reach the World Series for the 11th time.

Game 1 • Sabathia vs Beckett

10-3

CLE	1	0	0		0	0	1		0	1	0	3 8 0
BOS	1	0	4		0	3	2		0	0	x	10 12 0

FRIDAY OCTOBER 12, 2007 • **FENWAY PARK** ◇◇◇◇◇◇

Game 2 • Carmona vs Schilling

13-6

CLE	1	0	0		3	1	1		0	0	0	0 7	13 17 0
BOS	0	0	3		0	3	0		0	0	0	0 0	6 10 0

SATURDAY OCTOBER 13, 2007 • **FENWAY PARK** ◆◇◇◇◇◇

Game 3 • Matsuzaka vs Westbrook

4-2

BOS	0	0	0		0	0	0		2	0	0	2 7 0
CLE	0	2	0		0	2	0		0	0	x	4 6 1

MONDAY OCTOBER 15, 2007 • **JACOBS FIELD** ◆◆◆◇◇◇

Game 4 • Wakefield vs Byrd

7-3

BOS	0	0	0		0	0	3		0	0	0	3 8 0
CLE	0	0	0		0	7	0		0	0	x	7 9 1

TUESDAY OCTOBER 16, 2007 • **JACOBS FIELD** ◆◆◆◆◇◇

Game 5 • Beckett vs Sabathia

7-1

BOS	1	0	1		0	0	0		2	3	0	7 12 0
CLE	1	0	0		0	0	0		0	0	0	1 6 1

THURSDAY OCTOBER 18, 2007 • **JACOBS FIELD** ◆◆◆◆◆◇◇

Game 6 • Carmona vs Schilling

12-2

CLE	0	1	0		0	0	0		1	0	0	2 6 2
BOS	4	0	6		0	0	0		0	2	x	12 13 0

SATURDAY OCTOBER 20, 2007 • **FENWAY PARK** ◆◆◆◆◆◆◇

Game 7 • Westbrook vs Matsuzaka

11-2

CLE	0	0	0		1	1	0		0	0	0	2 10 1
BOS	1	1	1		0	0	0		2	6	x	11 15 1

SUNDAY OCTOBER 21, 2007 • **FENWAY PARK** ◆◆◆◆◆◆◆

Comeback

KINGS

The game was played on the 32nd anniversary of Carlton Fisk's World Series walkoff homer and though the score indicated little drama, the final play was no less spectacular. ♦ At 11:56 p.m. October 21, Casey Blake hit a towering shot toward the 420-foot sign in the deepest part of center field at Fenway Park. The ball descended from the October sky and settled into the outstretched mitt of a galloping Coco Crisp, who crashed into the bullpen fence and dropped to the ground holding the American League pennant in his hand. ♦ Completing a comeback from a 3-1 series deficit, the Red Sox won their 11th pennant with an 11-2 thrashing of the Cleveland Indians. Japanese rookie Daisuke Matsuzaka picked up the victory with five innings of solid pitching and fellow rookie Dustin Pedroia (home run, double) knocked in five runs as the Sox blew it open with eight runs in the seventh and eighth innings. Dating to the historic sweep of the Yankees in 2004, it marked the seventh straight ALCS elimination game

  won by the Red Sox. ♦ "It's the biggest event of my life," said Pedroia. ♦ "This team is appealing for a lot of reasons and that's a good sign for Red Sox Nation," said Sox CEO Larry Lucchino. "Home-field advantage has never meant as much as it does to me right now." ♦ And so the Sox advanced to the World Series for the second time in four years, which hasn't happened since James Michael Curley and George Herman Ruth prowled the narrow streets of Boston. ♦ Clearly, these Red Sox fear no team and no situation. Faced with three consecutive must-win games, Boston outscored Cleveland by an aggregate, 30-5. ♦ This must have been what it felt like in the early days of Fenway when the Royal Rooters ruled and the Red Sox were regular hosts of baseball's autumnal showcase. From 1915 through 1918, the Sox won three World Series. They did not win again until 2004, the beginning of a magical October run that has resumed over the last four days. ♦ On the heels of back-to-back wins in which the Sox outscored the Tribe, 19-3, fans came to Fenway expecting to see › PAGE 39

KEVIN YOUKILIS AND ERIC HINSKE REVEL IN WINNING THE PENNANT.

◆ A L C S 1 ◆

As Boston's hitters racked
up eight runs off the Indians'
C.C. Sabathia in less than
five innings, Red Sox ace
Josh Beckett held Cleveland
to just two runs in six
innings as the Sox rolled to a
10-3 victory in Game 1.

A L C S 1

Kevin Youkilis crossed the plate three times for Boston with a pair of singles and a walk. Meanwhile, Manny Ramirez walked three times and singled twice, driving in three runs while adding a fielding gem (below). Ramirez picked Asdrubal Cabrera's liner off his shoetops in the eighth inning.

FROM 34 • another champagne celebration on the Fenway lawn. Former Sox slugger Kevin Millar, a fabled member of the '04 champs, was flown in to toss the ceremonial first pitch, but fans were more concerned with the throwing skills of Matsuzaka, the $103-million man who failed in his first two postseason appearances.

While Matsuzaka threw his final warm-up pitches just after 8 o'clock, the Dropkick Murphys performed "I'm Shipping Up To Boston" from a temporary stage on the dirt adjacent to the Sox bullpen. The crowd roared when a team of Irish step dancers emerged from the center-field door and hopped up on stage. It was a pretty safe bet Dice-K never saw such a demonstration before any games he pitched against the Nippon Ham Fighters.

Showing none of the nervousness that marked his first two October starts, Matsuzaka mowed down the Tribe in the first inning on 13 pitches. It was 9:30 Monday morning in Japan.

Good fortune walked with the Sox against Jake Westbrook in the first when a would-be double-play one-hopper bounced crazily off the infield dirt and clanged off the glove of shortstop Jhonny Peralta to give Manny Ramírez an RBI single.

The Sox made it 2-0 in the second when Jason Varitek led off with a Wall double, took third on a single by Jacoby Ellsbury, then scored on a double play grounder by Julio Lugo.

There was a moment of infamy for Cleveland's third base coach, Joel Skinner, in the seventh. Kenny Lofton was on second with one out after Lugo dropped a popup in shallow left.

Franklin Gutierrez followed with a shot over the third-base bag that bounded off the wall in foul territory. Ramírez had no shot at getting Lofton at home, but Skinner held the speedster at third. Naturally, Casey Blake followed with a double-play grounder and Cleveland fans had new reason to believe in the Curse of Rocky Colavito.

Pedroia crushed a two-run homer into the Monster seats off reliever Rafael Betancourt in the seventh, then cleared the bases with a two-out double in the eighth to erase all doubt.

ALCS 1

Reserve outfielder Bobby Kielty got the nod in right field because of his success vs. Cleveland starter Sabathia, and Kielty delivered a two-run single to the Boston cause.

David Ortiz (far left, with Mike Lowell) played the rare role of table setter in Game 2, reaching base all five times with two singles, two walks, and a hit-by-pitch. He also scored a pair of runs (above). Lowell (top) contributed a two-run double as the Sox grabbed a 5-1 lead in the third inning.

ALCS 2

Boston rallied twice to lead Game 2, but Red Sox starter Curt Schilling (right) and his relief corps failed to hang on. Schilling left in the fifth inning after surrendering five runs, and Manny Delcarmen (top right) allowed the Indians to tie the game at 6. The epic 5-hour, 14-minute game was lost in a seven-run Cleveland 11th inning, when Eric Gagne (top left) and Javier Lopez (above right) struggled. Grady Sizemore slid home well after 1 a.m. with the eventual winning run.

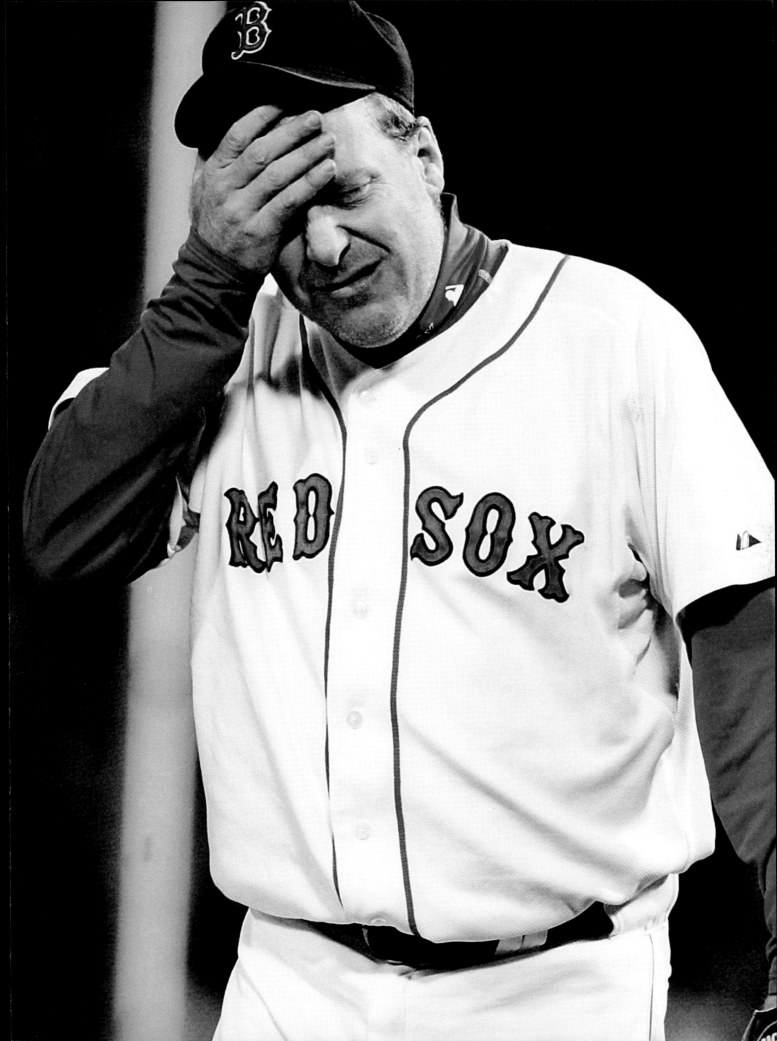

◆ A L C S ③

The series moved to Cleveland, and the Indians moved ahead, 2 games to 1. J.D. Drew's leap (far left) was too late to snag Kenny Lofton's two-run homer, and Dustin Pedroia made a pair of valiant bids that came up shy: Asdrubal Cabrera's ground ball eluded him (above) for a Cleveland run, and his bid to turn a double play (left) resulted in only a forceout and a run scored for Cleveland in their 4-2 win.

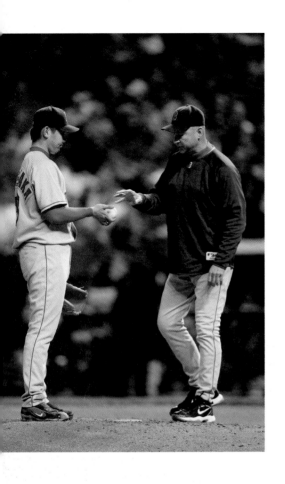

 ALCS 3

Manager Terry Francona takes the ball from Daisuke Matsuzaka (above) after Dice-K failed to finish the fifth inning of Game 3. Jacobs Field was turning into an inhospitable place for the Red Sox, who managed just seven hits and bounced into three double plays in the 4-2 defeat.

ALCS 4

Kevin Youkilis juggles the ball but is still able to get the out in the third inning (top left); then, in the fifth, he gets tangled up with Dustin Pedroia and drops a foul popup (bottom left). Coco Crisp flips his helmet after he was retired on a fly ball to end the sixth inning.

 ALCS 4

Outfielders (from left) Grady Sizemore, Kenny Lofton, and Franklin Gutierrez celebrate the Indians' third straight victory and a 3-1 series lead. Each of the three scored a run in the 7-3 win.

Manny Ramirez saw no reason not to celebrate his long-gone home run in the sixth inning, a solo shot that trimmed the Indians' lead to four runs, 7-3. About Manny's reaction to the shot, teammate Mike Lowell said, "I don't understand that one, but that's him."

Try as he might, Cleveland center fielder Grady Sizemore is unable to reach a drive by Manny Ramirez that hit the top of the wall for a single (left), and Sizemore can only deflect a ball off the bat of Kevin Youkilis that went for a triple (above) and an RBI in the seventh inning.

ALCS 6

Boston's Dustin Pedroia
is safe at second base
with a double off Indians'
starter Fausto Carmona as
Cleveland's Asdrubal Cabrera
fails to come up with the ball.
The Sox rocked Carmona
for seven runs in two-plus
innings.

J.D. Drew drives a 3-2 pitch from Cleveland's Fausto Carmona into the center-field bleachers for a grand slam in the first inning. The Sox were in danger of squandering a bases-loaded, none-out chance when Drew delivered with two outs.

 ALCS 6

Staked to a big early lead, Boston Game 6 starter Curt Schilling kept Cleveland hopes dim by pitching seven innings of two-run ball. Schilling struck out five Indians while issuing no walks.

 ALCS 7

Hideki Okajima's delivery
kept the Indians off-balance
as he worked a pair of
scoreless innings. Although
Okajima gave up a pair of
hits to open the Cleveland
eighth inning, Jonathan
Papelbon came in to record
a six-out save.

Dustin Pedroia gave the Red Sox a little breathing room in the seventh inning with a two-run homer that barely cleared the Green Monster and put Boston up, 5-2. The Sox added seven runs in the eighth inning to turn the game into a rout.

 A L C S 7

Kenny Lofton's left hand appeared to beat the tag by Dustin Pedroia, but Lofton was ruled out on an assist from left fielder Manny Ramirez in the fifth inning. The call proved critical, because the Indians added a pair of singles after Lofton was erased, but managed only one run and still trailed, 3-2. They never scored again.

After an outstanding running catch by Coco Crisp ended the game, the team bounded to the middle of the field to celebrate the American League pennant. The Red Sox became just the 11th team out of 66 in baseball postseason history to win a series after trailing, 3 games to 1.

The Red Sox were clicking on all cylinders as they rode the shutout pitching of Josh Beckett and Curt Schilling and the long balls of Manny Ramirez & Co. into their third ALCS in five seasons.

Game 1 · Lackey vs Beckett

4-0

LA	0	0	0		0	0	0		0	0	0	0 4 0
BOS	1	0	3		0	0	0		0	0	x	4 9 0

WEDNESDAY OCTOBER 3, 2007 · **FENWAY PARK** ◈◇◇

Game 2 · Escobar vs Matsuzaka

6-3

LA	0	3	0		0	0	0		0	0	0	3 7 0
BOS	2	0	0		0	1	0		0	0	3	6 6 1

FRIDAY OCTOBER 5, 2007 · **FENWAY PARK** ◈◈◇

Game 3 · Schilling vs Weaver

9-1

BOS	0	0	0		2	0	0		0	7	0	9 10 0
LA	0	0	0		0	0	0		0	0	1	1 8 0

SUNDAY OCTOBER 7, 2007 · **ANGELS STADIUM** ◈◈◈

Heavenly

SWEEP

ANAHEIM, Calif. -- It was a frat party run amok, a band of delirious baseball brothers who raucously celebrated as if they had won the World Series. ♦ The Boston Red Sox unabashedly partied like it was 2004 after thrashing the Los Angeles Angels of Anaheim, 9-1, to complete a thoroughly humiliating sweep of the best the West had to offer. ♦ As the smell of sweat and champagne wafted throughout Boston's clubhouse, the Red Sox let loose, hugging and shouting and dancing to the heavy beat of their victory tunes. Kevin Youkilis, clad in royal blue swim goggles, screamed with delight as he doused Mike Lowell with a champagne and Budweiser cocktail. Jonathan Papelbon screeched like a little kid with a liquor license, tormenting anyone and everyone in his path with a bath of liquid refreshments. ♦ David Ortiz, who knocked yet another ball out of the park in the final game, traded some elbow high-fives, then quickly donned a rain poncho

  and retreated to the back of the room. Manny Delcarmen grabbed his own bottle of bubbly and promptly poured it down Papelbon's pants. ♦ General manager Theo Epstein, who on this day did not have to answer questions about J.D. Drew's production or Eric Gagne's price tag, smiled broadly and proclaimed, "This is fun. The guys have worked so hard …" ♦ Slugger Manny Ramirez interrupted Epstein's victory speech by drenching the young GM with a bucket full of ice water. With no Gatorade readily available, it was the next-best thing to the well-known postgame tradition. ♦ With the Angels safely eliminated, the Red Sox happily put the playoff button on pause for a moment to enjoy their accomplishments. The beauty of these celebrations is it doesn't matter whether you were a playoff hero or a playoff scrub. Kyle Snyder and Curt Schilling were indistinguishable in the madness that unfolded after the game. Both were soaked in alcohol, and mobbed by teammates. ♦ Who could help but notice Jon Lester › PAGE 70

KEVIN YOUKILIS
SOAKS IN THE VICTORY THAT ADVANCED
BOSTON TO THE ALCS.

 A L D S 1

Angels starter John Lackey (above) found the going rough in the third inning of Game 1 as the Red Sox scored three times en route to a 4-0 win. Meanwhile, Josh Beckett (right) found plenty to celebrate in his efficient four-hit shutout, in which he fanned eight and walked none while throwing 108 pitches.

FROM 66 • quietly taking it all in, knowing one year ago at this time his life — never mind his baseball future — was so cloudy because of a shocking cancer diagnosis? And there was Delcarmen, who grew up idolizing the team of his native city, who shuttled back and forth to Pawtucket wondering if he would ever get his chance to prove he belonged in the big leagues.

"I'm living my dream right now," he said. "All I ever wanted was to play for the Boston Red Sox, to have a chance to be in a playoff series. It's even sweeter, too, because I'm here with Pap [Papelbon] and [Dustin] Pedroia. We were in the minors together, hoping for the day something like this would happen to us."

Red Sox owner John Henry visited the clubhouse and offered his congratulations to his ball club, upon which he, too, was subjected to a victory bath of Bud and bubbly. Asked to characterize his team, the owner answered, "Relentless. That's the word that came up today. The lineup we had out there was so perfect. When you drop Manny back into that four spot, behind Ortiz and ahead of Mike Lowell, I can't imagine anything better. And Schilling - every pitch sequence was so crisp. It was a joy to watch.

"This group totally reminded me of the teams from 2003 and 2004. But even those teams didn't have this kind of bullpen."

There are a number of alumni from the 2004 championship team — Ortiz, Ramirez, Schilling, Jason Varitek, Tim Wakefield, Youkilis, Mike Timlin, and Doug Mirabelli — but there are also a collection of kids who have heard all about the World Series wins, but were itching to create their own memories.

"It's a beautiful scene," said Papelbon, in between ripping open beers with his teeth. "It is what all of us have been working toward. And now we're here, and for a little while, at least, we're going to have some fun."

 ALDS 1

Kevin Youkilis (left) jump-started the series offensively for Boston with a solo first-inning home run. Julio Lugo (above) erased the Angels' Howie Kendrick on a force play in the eighth inning.

The bat is suspended in mid-air as Manny Ramirez follows the flight of his game-winning homer off Angels' closer Francisco Rodriguez in the bottom of the ninth inning of Game 2. Rodriguez made his exit, while Ramirez accepted a low-five from his team's closer, Jonathan Papelbon, who earned the victory with 1 1/3 innings of hitless relief.

TEAMMATES CONVERGE ON MANNY RAMIREZ AS HE APPROACHES HOME PLATE AFTER FINALLY ENDING A 4-HOUR, 5-MINUTE GAME 2 WITH HIS WALK-OFF THREE-RUN HOMER.

Jacoby Ellsbury (right) leaps to spear a drive off the bat of the Angels' Orlando Cabrera in the eighth inning of the clinching 9-1 victory over the Angels. Curt Schilling (far right) finishes his seven shutout innings with a strikeout of Mike Napoli. Schilling allowed six hits and one walk while striking out four.

 ALDS 3

As the Angels' fortunes sagged, Red Sox fans filled the seats behind the Boston dugout. David Ortiz (below left) and Manny Ramirez (right) provided early signs that this series was sweepable, as their consecutive home runs in the fourth inning off Angels' starter Jared Weaver staked the Sox to a 2-0 lead.

After taking the division lead on April 18, the Red Sox wavered, but never surrendered first place and won the AL East for the first time since 1995, breaking a nine-year Yankee reign.

April
16-8
Josh Beckett starts season 5-0, and Red Sox start with a month that includes three-game sweep of the Yankees.

May
20-8
A fast Boston start combined with early struggles for the Yankees gives the Red Sox an 11.5-game advantage on May 29. Beckett improves to 8-0.

June
13-14
The Sox suffer four-game and three-game losing streaks, while also losing two of three to Yankees and Rockies. Sox also swept in Seattle.

July
15-12
Up-and-down month with five-game winning streak and two three-game losing skids is highlighted by back-to-back 1-0 games in Cleveland. Sox win first and lose second.

Aug.
16-13
Red Sox follow four-game sweep of White Sox (Boston outscores Chicago 46-7) by being swept by Yankees in three games to close the month.

Sept.
16-11
Rookie pitcher Clay Buchholz throws no-hitter in his second major league start. On Sep. 28, Sox capture their first division crown in 12 years.

Standings

EAST	W	L	PCT	GB
Boston	96	66	.593	–
New York	94	68	.580	2
Toronto	83	79	.512	13
Baltimore	69	93	.426	27
Tampa Bay	66	98	.407	30

How the
EAST
was won

September 29, 2007 • BY GORDON EDES/Globe Staff

Theo Epstein trusted that the Red Sox would hold up their end of a championship bargain, but thought it was a good idea to send a text message to Kevin Millar, exhorting the former Sox partymeister to help put an end to Yankee aspirations in Baltimore. ♦ "I told him, 'You own (Yankees pitcher Mike) Mussina, I said, 'You owe us one,'" Epstein said. "You've got to win at least one game for us singlehandedly. And tell (Orioles manager Dave)Trembley I don't want to see (Triple A) Ottawa out there." ♦ "He wrote back, 'We'll see what we can do. I'll do my best for you.'" ♦ It was the prelude to a made-for-TV experience. The Red Sox, 5-2 winners over the Minnesota Twins in a game that ended at 9:39 p.m., became champions of the American League East an hour and 17 minutes later, at 10:56, when Millar and the Orioles beat the Yankees, 10-9, in 10 innings, a comeback win the Sox watched from inside their clubhouse while several thousand fans watched on the Fenway Park video scoreboard. ♦ Millar did

his part, getting hit by a pitch by Yankees closer Mariano Rivera in the ninth, when the Orioles rallied from three runs down to tie the score on a bases-loaded triple by former Sox outfielder Jay Payton. A third ex-Sox player, Chad Bradford, was the winning pitcher after escaping a bases-loaded jam in the 10th, and Melvin Mora dropped a two-out squeeze bunt to bring home the winning run after Millar looked at a called third strike. ♦ Naturally, the irrepressible Millar was heard from in the midst of a wild Sox celebration that reached its apex when Alex Cora took command of the Fenway Park sound system, blasting "Sweet Caroline" while Jonathan Papelbon, wearing sliding shorts and a T-shirt, did a mad Irish jig on the mound. ♦ "He texted me back and said, 'I told you, I'd come through for you,'" Epstein said. "He said, 'I'm still sitting on that changeup, by the way. Congratulations." ♦ The Sox had not won a division title since 1995, and ended a run of nine straight division titles by the Yankees.

DAVID ORTIZ AND JONATHAN PAPELBON
CELEBRATE BOSTON'S FIRST
AMERICAN LEAGUE EAST TITLE IN 12 YEARS.

DICE-MAN COMETH 12/14/06

The Red Sox spent $103.1 million to acquire right-handed pitcher Daisuke Matsuzaka (right) from the Seibu Lions of the Japan League. General manager Theo Epstein negotiated the $52-million, six-year contract that brought "Dice-K" to Boston, which barely topped the $51.1-million posting fee the Sox paid the Lions just to talk with Matsuzaka.

DIMINUTIVE DUSTIN PEDROIA TAKES LOW FIVES FROM HIS TEAMMATES BEFORE THE SEASON OPENER.

OPEN SEASON 4/2/07

Curt Schilling (below) suffered his earliest exit from a regular-season game in 10 years, working only four innings of the Royals' 7-1 victory in the season opener at Kansas City. Tony Pena Jr., son of the former Sox catcher, had two triples to help send Boston to its sixth loss in its last seven season openers.

DICE-K ROLLS 4/5/07

It seemed as though it
would be impossible for
Daisuke Matsuzaka to live
up to the expectations
that accompanied his first
Red Sox start, but he did.
Throwing 108 pitches,
Dice-K struck out 10 Royals
and allowed only one run on
six hits over seven innings
of a 4-1 victory at Kauffman
Stadium. That heightened
the excitement when he
debuted at Fenway (above)
the following week.

HOME OPENER 4/10/07

On a biting, breezy Opening Day, Josh Beckett (right), often overshadowed in spring training amid the Dice-K mania, gave up a run and two hits over seven innings and retired the final 15 batters he faced in a 14-3 victory over the Seattle Mariners. "Very, very impressive, from start to finish," offered manager Terry Francona.

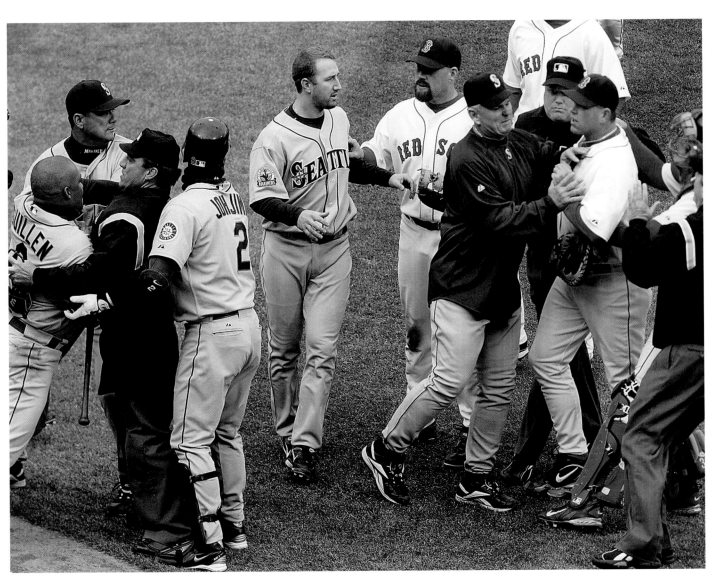

ABOVE: BENCHES EMPTY AS PLAYERS, COACHES, AND UMPIRES RESTRAIN SEATTLE'S JOSE GUILLEN AND BOSTON PITCHER BRENDAN DONNELLY DURING THE SEASON OPENER AT FENWAY.

LOCAL DEBUT 4/11/07

In his first Fenway start, Daisuke Matsuzaka (left, with catcher Jason Varitek) pitched well, but was upstaged by Seattle's Felix Hernandez. The 21-year-old threw a one-hitter to give the Mariners a 3-0 win. J.D. Drew's single to open the eighth inning was Boston's lone hit. Matsuzaka did manage to retire Ichiro Suzuki all four times he faced him.

LEFT: JULIO LUGO ROBS THE ANGELS OF A HIT IN THE FOURTH INNING OF THIS APRIL 16 GAME.

THE BIG SWEEP 4/20-22/07

In the third inning of a 7-6 conquest of the Yankees, the Red Sox hit back-to-back-to-back-to-back homers off rookie Chase Wright. Manny Ramirez, J.D. Drew, Mike Lowell, and Jason Varitek (bottom left) became the fifth quartet in baseball history to pull off the feat, and Boston went on to sweep the three-game set. The Sox trailed by at least two runs in all three victories. The result was all the sweeter because the Bronx Bombers' previous trip to Fenway had been a five-game trampling of the Red Sox in August 2006. It was the first time the Sox swept a series of at least two games against the Yankees at home since 1990. Photos at left include Johnny Damon getting razzed and Jason Varitek sliding home in Game 1, Jonathan Papelbon sealing the win in Game 2, and Dustin Pedroia going flat out to catch a ball in Game 3.

91

DUSTIN PEDROIA FLIES HIGH TO TURN A DOUBLE PLAY IN A 13-4 WIN OVER
THE BALTIMORE ORIOLES ON MAY 12 AT FENWAY.

DREW HITS WALL 5/15/07

Eyebrows were raised when the Sox paid $70 million for free agent J.D. Drew, no stranger to the disabled list in his bumpy career. With expectations high, the unemotional Drew didn't impress fans much out of the gate. Then he literally hit the wall in May (right), injuring his back while trying to prevent a home run by Detroit's Brandon Inge. Drew wouldn't get back on track until September.

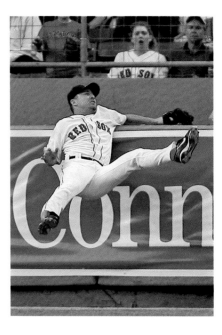

OKEY DOKEY START

Hideki Okajima gave up a homer on his first big-league pitch, but it turned into a much smoother ride, including an unexpected spot on the AL All-Star team. "Okie" admittedly clicked on his own name 10 times in the online voting, but his unique delivery, streak of scoreless innings, and 0.83 ERA had a lot more to do with the honor.

NEAR NO-HITTER 6/7/07

One out away, and Oakland's Shannon Stewart lined a clean single off Curt Schilling (above). The 425th start of Schilling's career would be his third one-hitter. More importantly for the Red Sox, who had lost their previous four games, Schilling delivered a 1-0 win, thanks to David Ortiz's first-inning home run.

LESTER'S LIFT 7/23/07

After a bout with cancer, Jon Lester wasn't daunted by the Indians' lineup. He turned in a remarkable start in his return to the majors (welcomed by fans, above), allowing two runs on five hits and three walks in a 6-2 triumph over one of the best teams in the league.

MR. LIGHTS OUT? 8/1/07

Reliever Eric Gagne (right) was all smiles when he first came to Boston, where he was expected to be a key piece of the team's stretch drive and postseason puzzle. Instead, he soon became a puzzle of his own, blowing key saves and watching his ERA balloon.

COCO CRISP AND HIS SHADOW BOTH MAKE THE CATCH ON AUG. 2.

A HOMECOMING 8/14/07

In a long career, Mike Lowell had hit just one home run in the bottom of the ninth to tie a ballgame. That his second one, on this night, should save a game started by fellow cancer survivor Jon Lester (above and right) was special, Lowell said, because it was Lester's first Fenway start of the season. Lester allowed Tampa Bay just a run on two hits in seven innings in Boston's 2-1 victory, which was assured by Coco Crisp's RBI single one out after Lowell's homer.

MANNY RAMIREZ
IS THE PICTURE
OF COOL BEFORE
THE START
OF THE ILL-FATED
SERIES.

BROOMED IN DA BRONX

KEVIN YOUKILIS AVOIDS THE TAG OF JASON GIAMBI, BUT THE SOX STILL DROPPED THEIR THIRD IN A ROW TO THE YANKEES.

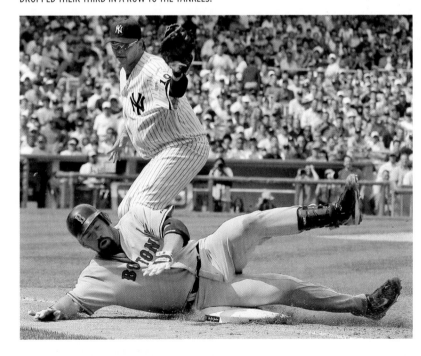

SWEPT BACK 8/28-30/07

Payback is... well, it isn't fun, as the Red Sox found in a late August visit to Yankee Stadium. New York won a pair of one-run games before blanking the Sox in the finale, 5-0, as Chien-Ming Wang allowed just one hit in seven innings, and the Yankees' Derek Jeter went 4-for-4.

TIMLIN'S FEAT 8/31/07

Mike Timlin became the 13th pitcher in baseball history to appear in 1,000 games on a night when the Red Sox would lose, 9-8, to the Orioles. Timlin heard cheers on the way to the mound, but was booed when he gave up four runs in two-thirds of an inning, including a homer by Nick Markakis (below left).

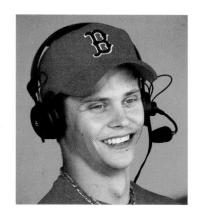

CLAY'S NO-HITTER 9/1/07

In only his second career start, Clay Buchholz, a right-hander from the East Texas town of Nederland, became the first Sox rookie to throw a no-hitter in a 10-0 win over the Orioles. Buchholz fanned Nick Markakis for the final out to send his teammates, led by David Ortiz, charging to the mound to engulf him. It was the first no-hitter by a Sox pitcher since Derek Lowe beat Tampa Bay in 2002.

JACOBY ELLSBURY SNAGS A SINKING LINE DRIVE BY BALTIMORE'S JAY PAYTON IN A 3-2 VICTORY ON SEPT. 2.

RARE SIGHTING 9/12/07

David Ortiz celebrates his second homer of the night and his first walk-off blast of the season, a two-run shot that gave the Red Sox a 5-4 win over the Devil Rays at Fenway Park. Ortiz drove in all of Boston's runs. It was his 10th walk-off home run in five seasons in Boston.

KEVIN YOUKILIS WRITHES IN PAIN AFTER BEING HIT ON THE RIGHT WRIST BY YANKEES PITCHER
CHIEN-MING WANG IN A 10-1 RED SOX WIN ON SEPT. 15.

20-GAME WINNER 9/21/07

With an 8-1 victory over Tampa Bay, Josh Beckett (right) became the first pitcher to win 20 games since 2005 and Boston's first since Curt Schilling in 2004. The native of Spring, Texas, also carved another notch toward fulfilling a youthful boast that he might one day be mentioned in the company of his heroes, Nolan Ryan and Roger Clemens (far left).

cap.com

9/22/07

Kevin Youkilis, Royce Clayton, and Manny Ramirez raise a cheer after Julio Lugo's dramatic two-run home run gave the Red Sox an 8-6 victory and sent them into the postseason for the 18th time in their history, and the fourth time in five years. Boston's win, coupled with Detroit's 7-4 loss to the Royals, clinched at least a wild-card spot with seven games left in the season.

devilra

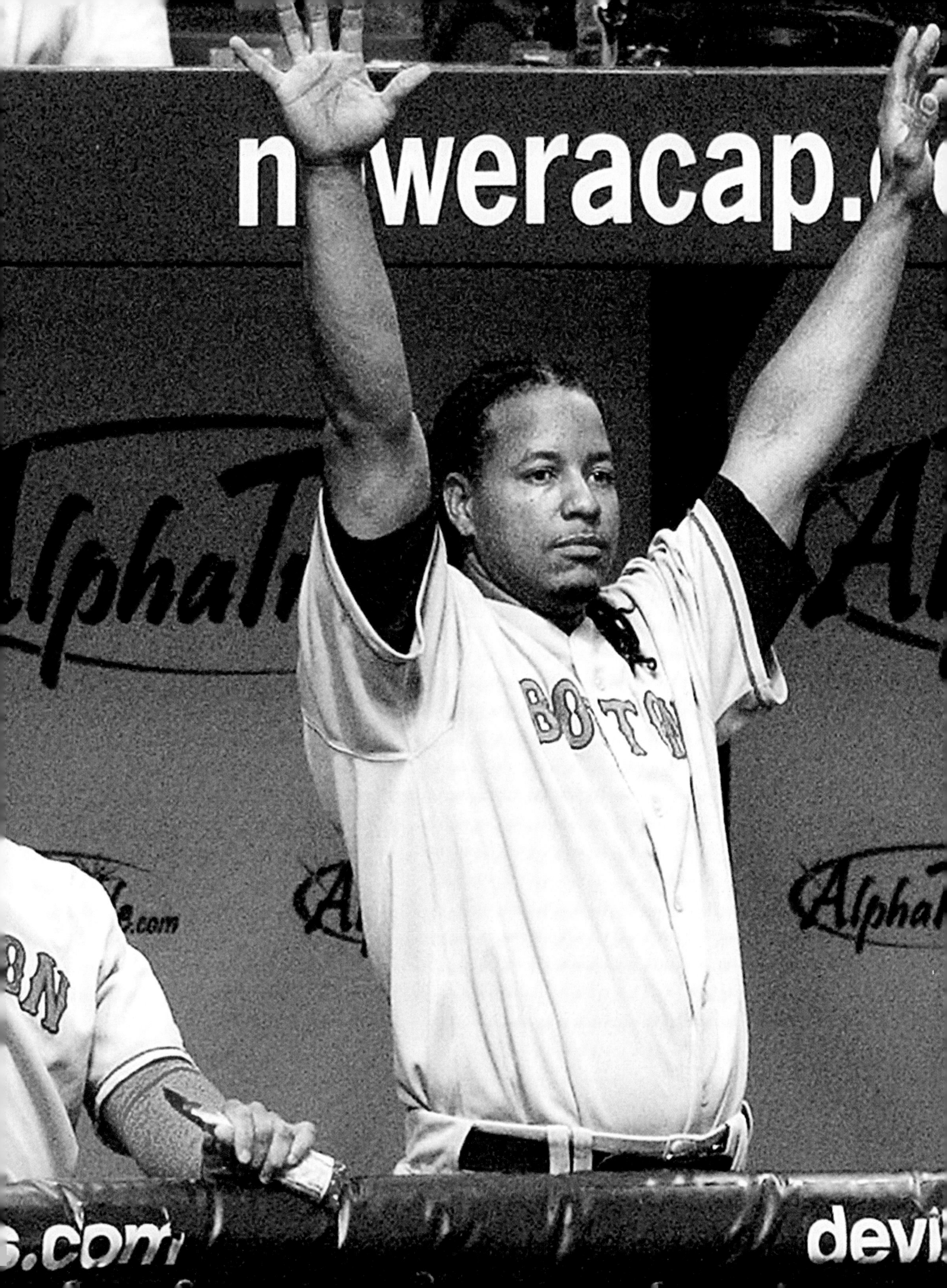

Beckett started the year 9-0 with two no-decisions; Matsuzaka started off 7-2 with one no-decision. Beckett only lost two games in a row once; Dice-K lost two straight once and three straight twice.

JOSH BECKETT

W	L	ERA	IP	H	ER	BB	SO
20	7	3.27	200.2	189	73	36	194

Date	Game	Dec	IP	H	ER	BB	SO
APR 4	@KC	W	5.0	2	1	4	5
APR 10	SEA	W	7.0	2	1	0	8
APR 16	LAA	W	6.0	6	1	1	5
APR 21	NYY	W	6.2	9	4	2	7
APR 26	@BAL	W	8.0	8	2	0	3
MAY 2	OAK	W	7.0	6	3	2	7
MAY 8	@TOR	W	7.0	5	1	1	5
MAY 13	BAL	ND	4.0	2	2	2	7
MAY 29	CLE	W	7.0	3	2	1	7
JUN 3	NYY	ND	6.1	8	4	3	5
JUN 8	@ARI	W	8.0	5	2	0	8
JUN 14	COL	L	5.0	10	6	1	1
JUN 19	@ATL	W	6.0	4	0	2	3
JUN 24	@SD	W	8.0	6	2	1	8
JUN 30	TEX	L	5.0	10	5	0	4
JUL 5	TB	W	6.0	9	3	1	9
JUL 15	TOR	L	8.0	7	2	2	8
JUL 20	CWS	W	6.0	4	3	2	10
JUL 25	@CLE	L	8.0	4	1	0	7
JUL 31	BAL	L	8.0	9	5	2	6
AUG 5	@SEA	W	6.2	8	1	2	9
AUG 11	@BAL	W	8.2	8	2	0	8
AUG 17	LAA	ND	7.0	5	1	1	8
AUG 24	@CWS	W	5.2	7	3	3	4
AUG 29	@NYY	L	6.2	13	4	1	6
SEP 4	TOR	W	8.0	5	3	2	7
SEP 9	@BAL	W	7.0	7	2	0	8
SEP 15	NYY	W	7.0	3	1	2	7
SEP 21	@TB	W	6.0	4	1	2	8
SEP 27	MIN	L	6.0	10	5	0	6

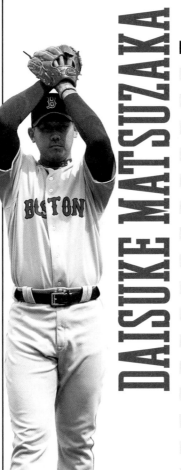

DAISUKE MATSUZAKA

W	L	ERA	IP	H	ER	BB	SO
15	12	4.40	204.2	191	100	80	201

Date	Game	Dec	IP	H	ER	BB	SO
APR 5	@KC	W	7.0	6	1	1	10
APR 11	SEA	L	7.0	8	3	1	4
APR 17	@TOR	L	6.0	3	2	3	10
APR 22	NYY	W	7.0	8	6	1	7
APR 27	@NYY	W	6.0	5	4	4	7
MAY 3	SEA	ND	5.0	5	7	5	1
MAY 9	@TOR	W	7.0	5	1	3	8
MAY 14	DET	W	9.0	6	1	0	5
MAY 19	ATL	W	8.0	9	3	0	6
MAY 25	@TEX	W	5.0	7	5	3	6
MAY 30	CLE	L	5.2	12	6	0	4
JUN 5	@OAK	L	7.0	7	2	2	8
JUN 10	@ARI	L	6.0	4	2	4	9
JUN 16	SF	W	7.0	3	0	3	8
JUN 22	@SD	W	6.0	5	1	5	9
JUN 27	@SEA	ND	8.0	3	1	1	8
JUL 3	TB	W	8.0	4	0	1	9
JUL 8	@DET	L	5.0	10	6	1	4
JUL 14	TOR	W	6.0	9	4	2	2
JUL 19	CWS	L	5.0	2	3	6	6
JUL 24	@CLE	W	7.0	4	0	3	5
JUL 29	@TB	L	6.1	8	2	1	6
AUG 4	@SEA	W	7.0	6	2	2	10
AUG 10	@BAL	ND	7.0	4	1	4	7
AUG 15	TB	L	6.0	8	6	3	5
AUG 22	@TB	L	6.0	2	2	4	8
AUG 28	@NYY	L	6.1	6	5	3	2
SEP 3	TOR	W	5.1	10	7	1	3
SEP 8	@BAL	L	2.2	6	8	3	2
SEP 14	NYY	ND	5.2	4	2	5	7
SEP 22	@TB	ND	6.2	6	5	3	7
SEP 28	MIN	W	8.0	6	2	2	8

2007

FACTS

&

figures

2007 REGULAR SEASON

DATE	OPPONENT	SCORE	PLACE	THE LOWDOWN
APRIL				
4/2	@ Kansas City	L 7-1	T-2nd ▼ 1	Schilling touched up for five runs in four innings.
4/4	@ Kansas City	W 7-1	T-2nd .5	Beckett goes five innings, giving up only one run.
4/5	@ Kansas City	W 4-1	1st ▲ .5	Dice-K debut: 7 IP, 1 ER, 10 Ks.
4/6	@ Texas	L 2-0	2nd ▼ .5	Tejeda holds Sox to two hits in 7 IP.
4/7	@ Texas	L 8-2	4th ▼ .5	Sosa homers and drives in two runs.
4/8	@ Texas	W 3-2	2nd ▼ .5	Schilling bounces back, giving up only one run.
4/10	Seattle	W 14-3	T-1st —	Beckett 7 IP, 1 ER. Drew and Varitek each 3 RBI.
4/11	Seattle	L 3-0	2nd ▼ 1	Hernandez one-hits Sox.
4/13	Los Angeles Angels	W 10-1	2nd ▼ .5	Wakefield goes 7 IP; Ortiz, Lowell three RBI each.
4/14	Los Angeles Angels	W 8-0	T-1st —	Schilling in command, goes eight innings.
4/16	Los Angeles Angels	W 7-2	1st ▲ .5	Beckett goes to 3-0 on Patriots Day.
4/17	@ Toronto	L 2-1	2nd ▼ .5	Dice-K strikes out 10 again.
4/18	@ Toronto	W 4-1	1st ▲ .5	Wakefield wins with seven innings of work.
4/19	@ Toronto	W 5-3	1st ▲ 1	Sox rally with four runs in the last two innings.
4/20	New York Yankees	W 7-6	1st ▲ 1.5	Sox score five in eighth inning.
4/21	New York Yankees	W 7-5	1st ▲ 1.5	Ortiz drives in four runs.
4/22	New York Yankees	W 7-6	1st ▲ 1.5	Lowell hits two homers, drives in four runs.
4/23	Toronto	L 7-3	1st ▲ 1.5	Hill goes 4-for-5 with two RBIs.
4/24	Toronto	L 10-3	1st ▲ 1.5	Wells, Thomas, Overbay combine for nine RBI.
4/25	@ Baltimore	W 6-1	1st ▲ 2.5	Schilling strong again, going seven innings.
4/26	@ Baltimore	W 5-2	1st ▲ 3	Beckett goes to 5-0 with eight innings of work.
4/27	@ New York Yankees	W 11-4	1st ▲ 4	Dice-K wins, giving up four runs in six innings.
4/28	@ New York Yankees	L 3-1	1st ▲ 3.5	Igawa throws six innings of shutout ball in relief.
4/29	@ New York Yankees	W 7-4	1st ▲ 4	Cora drives in three runs.
MAY				
5/1	Oakland	L 5-4	1st ▲ 3.5	Buck homers off Papelbon for tie, then A's win in 10.
5/2	Oakland	W 6-4	1st ▲ 4.5	Beckett wins sixth, going seven innings.
5/3	Seattle	W 8-7	1st ▲ 5.5	Ramirez hits two homers as Dice-K struggles.
5/4	@ Minnesota	W 2-0	1st ▲ 6.5	Wakefield gives up three hits in seven innings.
5/5	@ Minnesota	L 2-1	1st ▲ 5.5	Twins bullpen allows no hits in four innings.
5/6	@ Minnesota	W 5-3	1st ▲ 5.5	Schilling strikes out seven.
5/8	@ Toronto	W 9-2	1st ▲ 6	Beckett gets seventh victory.
5/9	@ Toronto	W 9-3	1st ▲ 6	Dice-K rebounds, gives up one run in seven IP.
5/10	@ Toronto	W 8-0	1st ▲ 7	Wakefield gives up no runs for second straight game.
5/11	Baltimore	L 6-3	1st ▲ 6	Tavarez shaky in disappointing outing.
5/12	Baltimore	W 13-4	1st ▲ 7	Sox score eight runs in final two innings.
5/13	Baltimore	W 6-5	1st ▲ 8	Sox score six in bottom of ninth.
5/14	Detroit	W 7-1	1st ▲ 8.5	Dice-K has complete game.
5/15	Detroit	L 7-2	1st ▲ 8	Ordonez drives in three runs.
5/17	Detroit	W 4-2	1st ▲ 9.5	Hinske makes saving catch and hits two run homer.
5/17	Detroit	W 2-1	1st ▲ 9.5	Tavarez wins, going seven innings.
5/19	Atlanta	W 13-3	1st ▲ 9.5	Dice-K goes six as Sox hit four homers.
5/19	Atlanta	L 14-0	1st ▲ 9.5	Braves get doubleheader split, pounding 18 hits.
5/20	Atlanta	W 6-3	1st ▲ 10.5	Gabbard debut a success: 5 IP, 2 ER.
5/21	@ New York Yankees	L 6-2	1st ▲ 9.5	Wakefield gives up six runs in five innings.
5/22	@ New York Yankees	W 7-3	1st ▲ 10.5	Ramirez hits three-run homer.
5/23	@ New York Yankees	L 8-3	1st ▲ 9.5	Pettitte outduels Schilling.
5/25	@ Texas	W 10-6	1st ▲ 10.5	Dice-K gives up seven runs in five innings.
5/26	@ Texas	W 7-4	1st ▲ 11	Sox score five in the sixth.
5/27	@ Texas	W 6-5	1st ▲ 11.5	Varitek hits three-run homer.
5/28	Cleveland	W 5-3	1st ▲ 11.5	Schilling strikes out 10 in seven innings.
5/29	Cleveland	W 4-2	1st ▲ 11.5	Beckett goes to 8-0.
5/30	Cleveland	L 8-4	1st ▲ 10.5	Byrd mows down Sox, Dice-K struggles.

DATE	OPPONENT	SCORE	PLACE	THE LOWDOWN
			JUNE	
6/1	New York Yankees	L 9-5	1st ♠ 10	Yankees score six off Wakefield in fourth.
6/2	New York Yankees	W 11-6	1st ♠ 11	Sox score eight in last three innings.
6/3	New York Yankees	L 6-5	1st ♠ 10.5	A-Rod homers off Papelbon in ninth.
6/4	@ Oakland	L 5-4	1st ♠ 10	Chavez hits game-winning HR in 11th off Snyder.
6/5	@ Oakland	L 2-0	1st ♠ 9	Ex-Sox player DiNardo shuts down former mates.
6/6	@ Oakland	L 3-2	1st ♠ 9	Wakefield gives up all runs in the fourth.
6/7	@ Oakland	W 1-0	1st ♠ 10	Schilling loses no-hitter after 8 2/3 innings.
6/8	@ Arizona	W 10-3	1st ♠ 10.5	Drew drives in seven as Beckett goes to 8-0.
6/9	@ Arizona	W 4-3	1st ♠ 10.5	Lowell drives in Ortiz to win in 10 innings.
6/10	@ Arizona	L 5-1	1st ♠ 9.5	Randy Johnson 6 IP, 9 Ks.
6/12	Colorado	W 2-1	1st ♠ 9.5	Wakefield solid in eight innings.
6/13	Colorado	L 12-2	1st ♠ 8.5	Helton drives in four as Schilling is shelled.
6/14	Colorado	L 7-1	1st ♠ 7.5	Beckett handed first loss.
6/15	San Francisco	W 10-2	1st ♠ 8.5	Pedroia goes 5 for 5, with 5 RBI.
6/16	San Francisco	W 1-0	1st ♠ 8.5	Manny homers as Dice-K deals eight solid innings.
6/17	San Francisco	W 9-5	1st ♠ 8.5	Ramirez drives in three; Bonds homers.
6/18	@ Atlanta	L 9-4	1st ♠ 8	Crisp goes 4-for-4, 2 RBI.
6/19	@ Atlanta	L 4-0	1st ♠ 9	Beckett bounces back, going six innings.
6/20	@ Atlanta	W 11-0	1st ♠ 10	Sox hit five home runs.
6/22	@ San Diego	W 2-1	1st ♠ 10.5	Dice-K-Papelbon combo frustrates Padres.
6/23	@ San Diego	L 6-1	1st ♠ 10.5	Young strikes out 11.
6/24	@ San Diego	W 4-2	1st ♠ 11	Beckett outduels Peavy with eight strong innings.
6/25	@ Seattle	L 9-4	1st ♠ 10	Weaver quiets Sox.
6/26	@ Seattle	L 8-7	1st ♠ 10	Sexson homer provides difference.
6/27	@ Seattle	L 2-1	1st ♠ 9	Sox swept in Seattle.
6/29	Texas	W 2-1	1st ♠ 10.5	Wakefield goes eight innings.
6/30	Texas	L 5-4	1st ♠ 10.5	Sosa gets 602nd homer.
			JULY	
7/1	Texas	L 2-1	1st ♠ 10.5	Loe confuses Sox hitters.
7/2	Texas	W 7-3	1st ♠ 10.5	Hinske triples and Pedroia has a two-run double.
7/3	Tampa Bay	W 4-1	1st ♠ 10.5	Dice-K tosses eight shutout innings.
7/4	Tampa Bay	W 7-5	1st ♠ 11.5	Lowell homers and scores two runs.
7/5	Tampa Bay	W 15-4	1st ♠ 11.5	Beckett goes to 12-2, Rays lose 11th straight.
7/6	@ Detroit	L 2-9	1st ♠ 10.5	Thames grand slam tames Sox.
7/7	@ Detroit	L 3-2	1st ♠ 10.5	Rodriguez gets game-winner in 13th.
7/8	@ Detroit	L 6-5	1st ♠ 9.5	Dice-K allows three home runs for the first time.
7/12	Toronto	W 7-4	1st ♠ 9.5	Wakefield beats Halladay.
7/13	Toronto	L 6-5	1st ♠ 9.5	Rios drives in winning run in the sixth.
7/14	Toronto	W 9-4	1st ♠ 9.5	Ortiz hits first homer at home since April.
7/15	Toronto	L 2-1	1st ♠ 8.5	Beckett goes eight in loss.
7/16	Kansas City	W 4-0	1st ♠ 8.5	Gabbard pitches complete game.
7/17	Kansas City	L 9-3	1st ♠ 7.5	Wakefield takes his ninth loss of the season.
7/18	Kansas City	L 6-5	1st ♠ 6.5	Butler doubles in go-ahead run in a four-run fifth.
7/19	Chicago White Sox	L 4-2	1st ♠ 6.5	Pierzynski goes 3-for-4 with a trio of RBIs.
7/20	Chicago White Sox	W 10-3	1st ♠ 7.5	Beckett pitches six solid innings, striking out 10.
7/21	Chicago White Sox	W 11-2	1st ♠ 7	Crisp matches his career high with five RBIs.
7/22	Chicago White Sox	W 8-5	1st ♠ 7	Ramirez drives in four runs.
7/23	@ Cleveland	W 6-2	1st ♠ 7	Lester returns from cancer with victory.
7/24	@ Cleveland	W 1-0	1st ♠ 7	Dice-K outduels Sabathia.
7/25	@ Cleveland	L 1-0	1st ♠ 6	Carmona outshines Beckett.
7/26	@ Cleveland	W 14-9	1st ♠ 7	Ramirez hits two homers.
7/27	@ Tampa Bay	W 7-1	1st ♠ 8	Wakefield goes six innings.
7/28	@ Tampa Bay	W 12-6	1st ♠ 9	Sox score six in 12th inning.
7/29	@ Tampa Bay	L 5-2	1st ♠ 8	D-Rays score all runs in seventh inning.
7/31	Baltimore	L 5-3	1st ♠ 7	Bedard gives up two hits, Ortiz homers twice.

DATE	OPPONENT	SCORE	PLACE	THE LOWDOWN
	AUGUST			
8/1	Baltimore	W 5-4	1st ♠ 7	Sox rally with four runs in the seventh.
8/2	Baltimore	W 7-4	1st ♠ 8	Mirabelli goes 3-for-3 with a go-ahead, RBI single.
8/3	@ Seattle	L 7-4	1st ♠ 7	Betancourt has a career-high four RBIs.
8/4	@ Seattle	W 8-3	1st ♠ 7	Matsuzaka pitches seven effective innings.
8/5	@ Seattle	W 9-2	1st ♠ 7	Beckett strikes out nine and Ramirez homers.
8/6	@ Los Angeles Angels	L 4-2	1st ♠ 6	Schilling gives up a homer to Izturis in the seventh.
8/7	@ Los Angeles Angels	L 10-4	1st ♠ 5	Matthews Jr. robs Boston's Crisp of a home run.
8/8	@ Los Angeles Angels	W 9-6	1st ♠ 6	Pedroia hits a tiebreaking homer in the seventh.
8/10	@ Baltimore	L 6-5	1st ♠ 5	Okajima loses first game as O's score in ninth.
8/11	@ Baltimore	W 6-2	1st ♠ 5	Beckett rolls to 15th victory.
8/12	@ Baltimore	L 6-3	1st ♠ 4	Millar and Tejada power O's.
8/13	Tampa Bay	W 3-0	1st ♠ 4	Wakefield and Papelbon combine on two-hitter.
8/14	Tampa Bay	W 2-1	1st ♠ 5	Crisp drives in game-winner in bottom of ninth.
8/15	Tampa Bay	L 6-5	1st ♠ 5	Sox score all runs in last three innings as rally falls short.
8/17	Los Angeles Angels	L 8-4	1st ♠ 5	Sox capitalize after six strong innings from Buchholz.
8/17	Los Angeles Angels	L 7-5	1st ♠ 5	Angels rally for three runs in the ninth off Gagne.
8/18	Los Angeles Angels	W 10-5	1st ♠ 5	Ortiz grand slam sparks Sox.
8/19	Los Angeles Angels	L 3-1	1st ♠ 4	Saunders takes a shutout into the eighth inning.
8/20	@ Tampa Bay	W 6-0	1st ♠ 5	Wakefield wins 15th.
8/21	@ Tampa Bay	W 8-6	1st ♠ 6	Crisp and Lugo each contribute two-run doubles.
8/22	@ Tampa Bay	L 2-1	1st ♠ 5.0	Jackson outduels Dice-K.
8/24	@ Chicago White Sox	W 11-3	1st ♠ 6	Beckett becomes MLB's first 16-game winner of 2007.
8/24	@ Chicago White Sox	W 10-1	1st ♠ 6.5	Ortiz homers twice and Youkilis adds a three-run shot.
8/25	@ Chicago White Sox	W 14-2	1st ♠ 6.5	Wakefield joins Beckett as the only 16-game winners.
8/26	@ Chicago White Sox	W 11-1	1st ♠ 7.5	Ortiz, Kielty, and Drew all homer to complete sweep.
8/28	@ New York Yankees	L 5-3	1st ♠ 7	Damon hits two-run home run.
8/29	@ New York Yankees	L 4-3	1st ♠ 6	Clemens beats Beckett.
8/30	@ New York Yankees	L 0-5	1st ♠ 5	Wang shuts down Sox on two hits.
8/31	Baltimore	L 9-8	1st ♠ 5	Timlin makes 1,000th career appearance.
	SEPTEMBER			
9/1	Baltimore	W 10-0	1st ♠ 5	Buchholz throws no-hitter.
9/2	Baltimore	W 3-2	1st ♠ 6	Okajima escapes a one-out jam in the eighth.
9/3	Toronto	W 13-10	1st ♠ 7	Every hitter in Boston's lineup has at least one hit.
9/4	Toronto	W 5-3	1st ♠ 7	Beckett earns 17th victory.
9/5	Toronto	L 6-4	1st ♠ 6	Okajima serves up a game-winning homer in the ninth.
9/6	@ Baltimore	W 7-6	1st ♠ 6.5	Varitek hits a pinch-hit RBI single in ninth for the win.
9/7	@ Baltimore	W 4-0	1st ♠ 6.5	Lester rolls to 4-0.
9/8	@ Baltimore	L 11-5	1st ♠ 5.5	Seven-run third, punctuated by a grand slam off Dice-K.
9/9	@ Baltimore	W 3-2	1st ♠ 5.5	Beckett wins 18th. Crisp delivers the game-winning hit.
9/10	Tampa Bay	L 1-0	1st ♠ 5	Schilling is very good, but Scott Kazmir is better.
9/11	Tampa Bay	W 16-10	1st ♠ 5	Youkilis grabs lead with a three-run triple in the sixth.
9/12	Tampa Bay	W 5-4	1st ♠ 5	Ortiz's second homer is a walk-off blast.
9/14	New York Yankees	L 8-7	1st ♠ 4.5	Yankees score six in the eighth to erase a five-run deficit.
9/15	New York Yankees	W 10-1	1st ♠ 5.5	Beckett stops Yanks to earn 19th win.
9/16	New York Yankees	L 4-3	1st ♠ 4.5	Jeter hits three-run homer off Schilling in the eighth.
9/17	@ Toronto	L 6-1	1st ♠ 3.5	Wakefield gives up two of Thomas's three homers.
9/18	@ Toronto	L 4-3	1st ♠ 2.5	Gagne gives up three runs in the eighth.
9/19	@ Toronto	L 6-1	1st ♠ 1.5	Adams hits grand slam off Papelbon.
9/21	@ Tampa Bay	W 8-1	1st ♠ 2.5	Beckett stops the bleeding by getting 20th victory.
9/22	@ Tampa Bay	W 8-6	1st ♠ 2.5	Sox clinch playoff berth as they score three in the ninth.
9/23	@ Tampa Bay	L 5-4	1st ♠ 1.5	Wakefield takes first-ever loss at Tampa.
9/25	Oakland	W 7-3	1st ♠ 3.0	Schilling gives up one run in six innings.
9/26	Oakland	W 11-6	1st ♠ 3.0	Lowell leads the way with five RBIs.
9/27	Minnesota	L 5-4	1st ♠ 2.0	Beckett denied 21st victory.
9/28	Minnesota	W 5-2	1st ♠ 3.0	Dice-K wins as Sox clinch first AL East title in 12 years.
9/29	Minnesota	W 6-4	1st ♠ 3.0	Wakefield earns 17th victory.
9/30	Minnesota	L 3-2	1st ♠ 2.0	Varitek hits his 17th homer in a meaningless loss.

2007 POSTSEASON

DATE	OPPONENT	SCORE	THE LOWDOWN
		ALDS	
10/3	Los Angeles Angels	W 4-0	Beckett pitches complete-game, four-hit, no-walk shutout.
10/5	Los Angeles Angels	W 6-3	Ramírez hits walkoff, three-run homer off Angels closer Rodriguez.
10/7	@ Los Angeles Angels	W 9-1	Seven-run uprising in the eighth drains whatever life was left in Angels.
		ALCS	
10/12	Cleveland	W 10-3	Beckett strikes out seven while allowing only two runs in six innings pitched.
10/13	Cleveland	L 13-6	Indians score seven runs in the 11th inning in a five-hour, 14-minute game.
10/15	@ Cleveland	L 4-2	Lofton's two-run homer off Matsuzaka sparks Tribe.
10/16	@ Cleveland	L 7-3	Indians score all runs in the fifth as Byrd baffles Sox hitters for five innings.
10/18	@ Cleveland	W 7-1	Beckett strikes out 11 over eight solid innings, tying a career postseason high.
10/20	Cleveland	W 12-2	Drew's first-inning grand slam gives Schilling all the support he would need.
10/21	Cleveland	W 11-2	Pedroia's two-run homer in the seventh sends the Red Sox to a 5-2 lead.
		WORLD SERIES	
10/24	Colorado	W 13-1	Beckett strikes out nine en route to his fourth win of the postseason.
10/25	Colorado	W 2-1	Boston's bullpen allows no runs in the contest.
10/27	@ Colorado	W 10-5	Matsuzaka becomes the first Japanese pitcher to win a World Series game.
10/28	@ Colorado	W 4-3	Lester gives up no runs in 5²/₃; Lowell and Kielty each hit solo shots.

2007 BOSTON RED SOX ROSTER

PITCHERS

19	Josh Beckett
54	Craig Breslow
61	Clay Buchholz
30	Matt Clement
41	Brian Corey
17	Manny Delcarmen
53	Brendan Donnelly
83	Eric Gagne
43	Devern Hansack
56	Craig Hansen
	Kyle Jackson
31	Jon Lester
48	Javier Lopez
	Jay Marshall
74	Edgar Martinez
18	Daisuke Matsuzaka
37	Hideki Okajima
58	Jonathan Papelbon
62	David Pauley
38	Curt Schilling*
39	Kyle Snyder
51	Julian Tavarez
50	Mike Timlin*
49	Tim Wakefield*

CATCHERS

36	Kevin Cash
72	George Kottaras
28	Doug Mirabelli*
33	Jason Varitek*

INFIELDERS

11	Royce Clayton
13	Alex Cora
12	Eric Hinske
25	Mike Lowell
23	Julio Lugo
15	Dustin Pedroia
20	Kevin Youkilis*

OUTFIELDERS

10	Coco Crisp
7	J.D. Drew
46	Jacoby Ellsbury
32	Bobby Kielty
44	Brandon Moss
24	Manny Ramirez*

DESIGNATED HITTER

34	David Ortiz*

* 2004 World Series team member

COACHES

47	**Terry Francona** (MANAGER)
2	Brad Mills (BENCH)
16	Luis Alicea (FIRST BASE)
35	DeMarlo Hale (THIRD BASE)
52	John Farrell (PITCHING)
29	Dave Magadan (HITTING)
57	Gary Tuck (BULLPEN)

GIMME A 'B'
The "K-Men" in the bleachers have Josh Beckett's number: nine strikeouts, four looking.

HIGH SIGN

A jogger runs under a Red Sox banner strung between MIT buildings on Memorial Drive. A 12-year-old fan from Maine has Big Papi on his mind.

TOP DOGS

A 5-year-old fan enjoys a hot dog on Yawkey Way before a Yankees game in September. Principal owner John Henry salutes the fans after the Series clincher at Coors Field.

WINNING RECIPE

A Columbus, Ohio, woman amends one of the signs after ALCS Game 5 at Jacobs Field, while fans at Fenway Park have their own messages to deliver at Game 7.

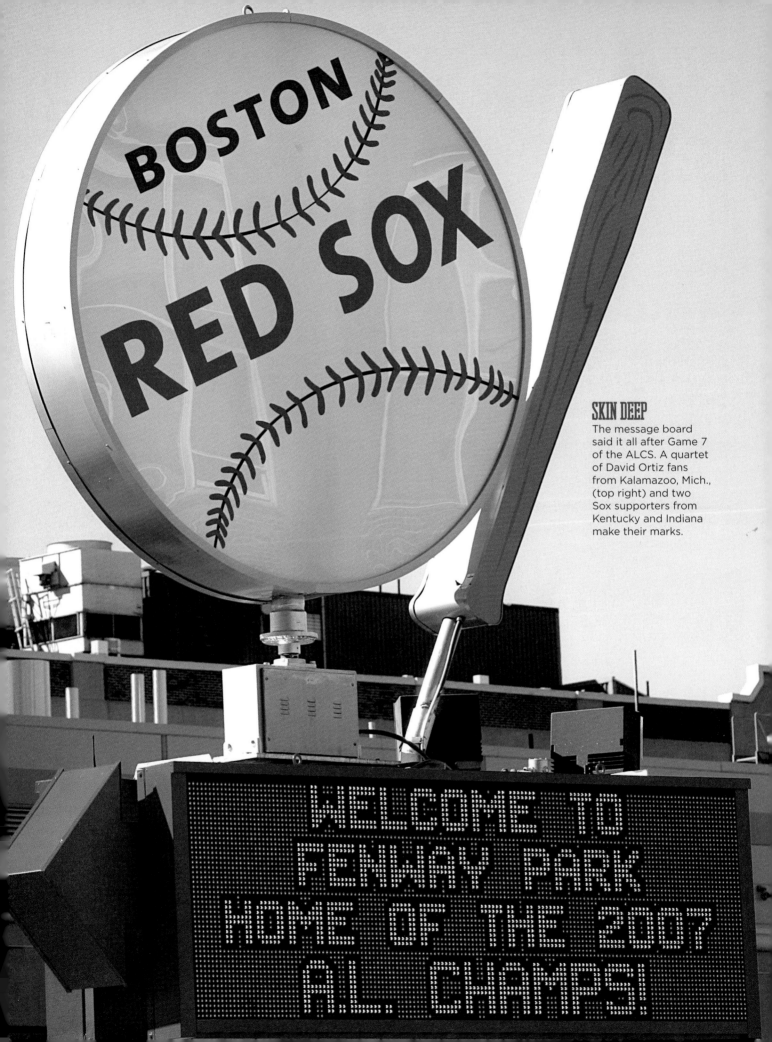

SKIN DEEP
The message board said it all after Game 7 of the ALCS. A quartet of David Ortiz fans from Kalamazoo, Mich., (top right) and two Sox supporters from Kentucky and Indiana make their marks.

BOSTON RED SOX

WELCOME TO FENWAY PARK HOME OF THE 2007 A.L. CHAMPS!

LAST DANCE
A fan holds a sign honoring Jonathan Papelbon's celebratory step dance while Papelbon was nailing down the final four outs of Boston's 2-1 win in Game 2 of the World Series.